WEATHER WONDERS

HEAT WAVES

HALEY WILLIAMS

PowerKiDS press

Published in 2027 by The Rosen Publishing Group, Inc.
2544 Clinton Street, Buffalo, NY 14224

First Edition

Book Design: Madison Thogmartin

Photo Credits: Cover, p. 1 Tom Wang/Shutterstock.com; p. 5 Ed Connor/Shutterstock.com; p. 7 Papa Papong/Shutterstock.com; p. 9 Guenter Albers/Shutterstock.com; p. 11 schankz/Shutterstock.com; p. 13 Quality Stock Arts/Shutterstock.com; p. 15 Oli_of_the_valley/Shutterstock.com; p. 17 Anurak Pongpatimet/Shutterstock.com; p. 19 People Images/Shutterstock.com; p. 21 Russamee/Shutterstock.com.

Cataloging-in-Publication Data
Names: Williams, Haley.
Title: Heat waves / Haley Williams.
Description: Buffalo, NY : Gareth Stevens Publishing, 2027. | Series: Weather wonders | Includes glossary and index.
Identifiers: ISBN 9781538295243 (pbk.) | ISBN 9781538295250 (library bound) | ISBN 9781538295267 (ebook)
Subjects: LCSH: Heat waves (Meteorology)--Juvenile literature.
Classification: LCC QC981.8.A5 W49 2027 | DDC 551.5253--dc23

Manufactured in China

CPSIA Compliance Information: Batch #QS27PK. For Further Information contact Rosen Publishing, at 1-800-237-9932.

CONTENTS

What Are Heat Waves?

A heat wave is a weather event. During a heat wave, the temperature is much higher than normal. The high heat level can last for days or weeks. It may even go on for months. Heat waves are very **dangerous**.

How Heat Waves Begin

A heat wave begins in Earth's **atmosphere**. High **air pressure** in the atmosphere pushes warm air down to the ground. The warm air continues being pushed down. It becomes trapped in an area. This creates a **dome** of heat.

With the warm air trapped, temperatures begin rising. There is not much wind. There are also fewer clouds to block the sun. This causes the temperature to feel even hotter. The ground also loses a lot of **moisture** during a heat wave. That makes the ground heat up more.

°C
°F
50
40
30
20
10
0
10
20
120
100
80
60
40
20
0

Climate Change

Heat waves can be caused by **climate** change. This is a long-term shift in Earth's temperatures. Changes in the climate can happen naturally. But since the 1800s, human activities have affected the climate. They have caused global temperatures to rise faster than normal.

Climate change can greatly affect weather events. These include heat waves. Higher world temperatures make heat waves more common. They can also cause a heat wave to last longer or be hotter. This affects people and the environment.

Damage

A heat wave can make the ground very dry. It can cause the ground to crack. Water becomes less available for animals and plants. This harms food crops. Fires are more likely to happen. And people use more electricity to stay cool. This may cause power to go out.

Heat waves can be dangerous for people's health. Very hot temperatures can cause heat-related illnesses. These can make a person's body temperature become too high. People might become **dehydrated**. They might pass out. People can even die.

Checking the Weather

Heat waves can happen anywhere. But they are most common in dry places. These include deserts. Experts **predict** heat waves using computers. They guess when and where a heat wave might occur. Then they can warn people who live in that area about it.

Staying Safe

People can prepare for heat waves. They can gather supplies, such as drinking water. Being inside can help people stay cool. If people go out, they should wear sunscreen. They should also stay in the shade and take breaks. Drinking lots of water is important, too.

GLOSSARY

air pressure: The weight of air pushing down on an area of Earth.

atmosphere: The layer of gases surrounding a planet.

climate: The typical weather pattern for an area over a long period of time.

dangerous: Likely to cause harm.

dehydrated: When a person does not have the normal amount of water in their body.

dome: Something shaped like half a ball.

moisture: Water or other liquids within an area or on a surface.

predict: To guess that something will happen in the future.

FOR MORE INFORMATION

BOOKS

Buckey, A.W. *Weather*. Minneapolis, MN: Abdo Publishing, 2025.

Crane, Cody. *Heat Waves*. New York, NY: Scholastic Inc., 2025.

WEBSITES

National Geographic Kids: Climate Change
kids.nationalgeographic.com/science/article/climate-change
Read about climate change at this website.

NESDIS: What Is a Heat Wave?
nesdis.noaa.gov/about/k-12-education/understanding-our-planet/what-heat-wave
Learn more about heat waves at this website.

INDEX